PLAY PRODUCTION

Practical Stage Handbooks

191

12

Practical Stage Handbooks
General Editor : HAROLD DOWNS

PLAY PRODUCTION

by
CONRAD CARTER

FOREWORD BY SIR DONALD WOLFIT, C.B.E.
PREFACE BY NORMAN MARSHALL

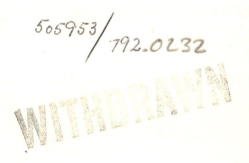
LONDON : HERBERT JENKINS

First Published by
Herbert Jenkins Ltd.
3 Duke of York Street,
London, S.W.1.
1953
Second Impression 1959

MADE AND PRINTED IN GREAT BRITAIN BY
WILLIAM CLOWES AND SONS, LIMITED, LONDON AND BECCLES

FOREWORD
by Sir Donald Wolfit, C.B.E.

THIS series of Practical Stage Handbooks is intended for those who have come to know the indefinable magic of the theatre. Their first experience of this may have arisen out of regular theatregoing, with memorable performances to give pleasure in recollection, or through personal work done to advance the Amateur Theatre.

This magic invariably stirs in the mind of the theatre-lover the desire for further knowledge of all the activities that contribute to the complex Art of the Theatre—acting, producing, costuming, make-up, lighting.

In schools and factories, in clubs and civic centres, interest that is created in the theatre is often followed by the determination to become a producer or a player, or to work "behind the scenes." But interest is not enough; knowledge is necessary. Some of this is, no doubt, acquired in haphazard fashion. The volumes in this Series will be of practical assistance to all to whom they are designed to appeal, thus adding knowledge to interest and strengthening what is often the irresistible magnetism of the theatre.

PREFACE

by NORMAN MARSHALL

I HAVE a profound respect for the good amateur producer. He achieves a successful production in the
face of difficulties unknown to his professional colleague.
He has to be a teacher as well as a producer. As the
author of this book points out, every amateur production is "a temporary School for Actors," while the
professional producer is continually developing his own
craft by learning from the skill and technique of the
more experienced members of his company.

The amateur producer usually rehearses with actors
already tired by their day's work, and who cannot be
expected to rehearse with the intense concentration of
the professional player whose livelihood in a fiercely
competitive profession may depend on the success or
failure of the show.

The fact that rehearsals of an amateur production are
often spread over a long period, with several days between each rehearsal, adds to the producer's difficulties,
as much time has to be spent in reminding the cast of
what was done in a scene which may not have been
rehearsed for a week or a fortnight. Often it is not
possible to rehearse upon the stage until the dress
rehearsal, and the stage itself may be of a size and shape
which would appal the professional producer.

Yet in spite of these difficulties and many others
which I have not enumerated, the standard of amateur
production steadily grows better. This is largely due to

7

the courses which are held for amateur producers, the criticism and advice of the better adjudicators at the drama festivals, the work of the county drama advisers, and the helpfulness of the books which have been written for the amateur producer. Here is another of these books, and one has a right to ask if it contains anything that has not already been said many times before, or whether it says it more clearly and incisively.

I think the particular excellence of this book is in the way the author instructs the producer how to plan each rehearsal so that he builds his production gradually and methodically, stage by stage. Amateur rehearsals are often messy and confused because the producer tries to cram far too much into every rehearsal.

There are many other matters over which I found myself enthusiastically agreeing with the author. For instance, his insistence on the proper distribution of emphasis in a sentence, so that the operative words are properly stressed. I often find amateur actors difficult to understand because in their anxiety to be audible they give equal importance to nearly every word, with the result that the sense of what they are saying is by no means clear. I agree with Mr. Carter that this is perhaps "the most common and glaring fault" of amateur acting, just as I agree with nearly everything else he has to say in this eminently clear and sensible book.

CONTENTS

AUTHOR'S NOTE

IN writing this book I have had in mind, primarily, amateur producers who have had little specialized training in production and whose opportunities for tuition are limited.

By many contacts with producers I have been convinced that what is most frequently lacking is a realization of the necessity for a *reason* underlying every movement and a *meaning behind* every spoken phrase. In other words, everything that happens on the stage must be *significant*—and co-ordination between speech and action is *vital*.

The next important necessity is to have an "ordered plan" based on sound artistic principles, a general framework in which production may be built up. If I have, in some measure, impressed these two necessities on my readers, much of the purpose of this book will have been achieved.

I take this opportunity of gratefully acknowledging the unfailing editorial guidance of Mr. Harold Downs and his kindly co-operation throughout, and my sincere thanks also to Mr. Norman Marshall for his most valuable and encouraging Preface.

C. C.

CHAPTER I

WHY A PRODUCER?

YOU are an amateur actor. You have decided to devote yourself to "production." I wonder why?

Perhaps you feel you have a "flair" for imparting knowledge. Or, perhaps, you are sure you will be more fully satisfied artistically if your function is to mould the whole play under your direction than if it is merely to play a single part in it. Or it may be that your drama group has no expert producer, cannot afford a professional, and possibly, in any event, would prefer to be directed by one of their own members than by a "stranger."

In addition, of course, some amateur actors have "taken up" production because (whether they admit it or not) they *enjoy* a position of domination and authority. I assume you are not one of these! This last is the very worst reason for attempting to become a producer.

Now another "Why?" Why producer at all? The most important reason is the simplest. No art can be practised successfully in a state of chaos—and chaos can be most alarmingly created in "putting on a play". This is easily realized if one considers four analogies applicable to a producer. A dramatist needs an interpreter. A class of students requires a teacher. A ship must have a captain. An orchestra must have a conductor. A play producer must be all of these.

I shall return to these analogies frequently since they are invaluable in illustrating his functions, knowledge, and responsibilities.

This book is not a treatise on advanced technique; nor will it be of much interest to the arty-and-crafty "'ism'-worshipper." It is intended for the sincere workaday craftsman whose heart and mind are in the essentials of his job; who desires to be a competent and successful producer of amateur actors, who, in their turn, wish to express themselves expertly in drama and to give good value for money to their audiences.

Whether your "group" is small, in, perhaps, a village or town, or a big society, in a city or an important area, is immaterial. The principles are the same. The fundamental knowledge, the direction and control, are equally necessary in each, and for their acquisition certain qualities are essential. These are: sincerity, artistic integrity, and that special kind of humility which does nothing to deprive its possessor of authority and respect.

The producer must be, frequently, an autocrat; not because he enjoys autocracy, but because it is in some degree indispensable to success. He must, however, be a diplomat who never mingles diplomacy with insincerity. He must have sympathy—yet forbear to suffer fools gladly; he must be a teacher—yet no pedant; he must be a captain—yet no tyrant. He must be a conductor who knows his score—and his orchestra.

This sounds as if he must be a super-man, but such an approach to perfection is rare! It is, however, toward this ideal that the producer must strive, if he is to do his best work, and extract from others the most satisfying artistic achievement.

It is for you to decide how far these personal qualities are inherent in your case, or to what degree you can acquire them. They must be stressed, as they are fundamental. But my chief business is to deal with knowledge, and how to employ it in every department and aspect of the producer's function.

I assume that you have at least average imagination, or vision, and react readily (yet not *too* readily!) to emotional conceptions, ideas, and expressions. Before these can be applied to the work in hand, considerable practical knowledge is demanded.

First, you must know how to read a play, not as a layman reads a novel, but as one who visualizes every word and every action in relation to their "projection." To prevent your conception becoming unduly "theatrical," the play must have been read already from another angle—as if it were the story of real people, recounted by someone who knew them; or, as if they were people intimately known to you. These two very different approaches to the play are of equal importance. Ultimate vision should be based on conviction and sympathy, together with realization of all the possibilities of stage treatment.

Play reading needs, first, a special approach, or combination of approaches, and then—experience. Intensive playreading will not have been restricted to those plays that happen to be under consideration by your group. Your past reading habits, your inherent talent for acting and training, will be of immense value to you as a reader of plays. The ability to read a play as a producer should read it is a highly important factor in his knowledge.

He must also have a knowledge of the mechanical resources and essential stage equipment, and how to employ them. Considerable theatrical knowledge can be gained from books. Time spent "back-stage," in a professional theatre or a "Little Theatre" run by experienced amateurs, will be of immense assistance. Offer your personal help in the performance of any tasks, however menial, and much practical knowledge will be picked up. Don't get in the way. Don't ask questions at busy moments. Work hard, await opportune moments, and you will have your reward. You will discover the true meanings of strange technical terms, and learn how the various contrivances are employed. You will see, too, how certain emotional effects are secured with the aid of lighting changes, scenery, furniture, and clothing—even the speed at which the curtain is lowered at the end of an act will be instructive. In short, you will remember what you have *read*, and see it applied in practice. Do not, however, fear that you will remain ignorant if you fail to get the entrée back-stage. In co-operation with your stage staff, you can set to work to apply the results of study for yourself. In certain circumstances this may be the better way.

You must have a knowledge of acting in all its aspects.

Do good actors make good producers? *Must* a producer be an actor?

Broadly speaking (I write of amateurs) producers should have some inherent talent for acting and have had some training. With reservations, I answer, "The better the actor, the better the producer"—but the reservations are important!

Actors whose training and experience have been principally as "straight juveniles" frequently fail as producers. They are prone to become "typed," and to lack imagination. Their technique is less flexible because the difference between one "juvenile lead" and another, though existent, is not so apparent as the frequent difference between one "character" part and another. One of the vices of acting is the tendency of "juveniles" to play every part alike, ignoring the fact that every author conceives a different person in his "juvenile" from any other, while the actor is prone to stamp each of these parts too deeply with his own personality, style, and mannerisms.

The best actor-producers are "character" actors. The essence of their job is the impersonation of a very *special* character—or, rather, a series of special characters in which imagination and observation of real life play a great part. He who can change himself from one to the other with relative ease is usually an artist whose technique is, by training and experience, flexible. If he is lucky (and wise), he does not become "typed." On the professional stage even "character" actors find their range limited by unavoidable circumstances—a fate the amateur can more easily evade.

The producer must be knowledgeable about the technique of acting, and, in his capacity of teacher, be able to impart his knowledge with confidence, authority, and speed. A brief thumb-nail sketch, a momentary "impersonation," are worth far more than ten minutes' academic dissertation.

He must have a sound grasp of stage lighting—he

need not be an expert electrician, for he will have technicians at his command—but he must know what lighting effects he requires, by what equipment, colours, intensities, and lighting angles they are achieved.

He must familiarize himself with the *décor*, furniture, properties, and costume of the period of the play, also with the movement, gestures, and manners of the time. Further, he must be something of an expert in make-up, able to teach and to do it. Every amateur actor should be well-trained in make-up, self-reliant, and need only the producer's check-over. In short, the cast must learn its job in every department of theatrecraft.

Although the aim is to make amateur actors as expert as professionals (so far as their inherent aptitudes and abilities permit!), the producer of an amateur group has special problems that do not face the producer of professionals—and vice-versa.

The professional producer has at his disposal a cast, each member of which has already acquired technical knowledge and skill. True, the knowledge and skill vary, but he is rarely, if ever, faced with an untrained and completely inexperienced actor. Therefore, in a broad sense, he is not required to "teach acting." His back-stage technicians are "professional," too, and thus his entire approach is different.

The personal, or social "atmosphere" differs between the professional and the amateur company. The bread and butter of professionals depend on their work. Amateurs work for the "love" of it—not, let us hope, for the mere "fun."

The artistic aim should be similar, but the approach in many respects must be different. Rehearsal procedure is different, too. Certain "rules and regulations," however, are common to both. They are willingly obeyed by professionals without any loss of dignity. There is no excuse for amateurs who will not submit to the same general principles of discipline, since they are vital to artistic success. It is for the producer to know what these are, their purpose, and to enforce them with understanding and tact, yet implacably.

CHAPTER II

THE PRODUCER AND HIS AUTHOR

THE producer is the interpreter of the author to the actor; therefore, it is manifest that he must "speak the author's language"—in other words, thoroughly understand the play and the author's intention.

The "dual approach" in reading a play, namely, the "real people" angle and the "stage presentation" conception has already been discussed. The producer's personal study of the play should be in this order, forgetting, first of all, about the theatre and that he is going to produce the play. It is even preferable, at this stage, if casting has not taken place, so that visualization shall not be coloured by pre-conceived ideas.

The play must be read with understanding and sympathy. If the producer finds himself quarrelling with the author, the passage must be read again and again; if he is still at variance, judgment must be suspended until the whole play has been read a second time. There are many dramatists, both celebrated and relatively unknown, the true qualities of whose work cannot be appraised fully, even by expert readers, at the first or even the fourth reading. Their plays "grow on" the reader rather than create an immediate, vivid impression. As an editor and "play doctor," I have read many such, and among what are now my favourite plays are a great number that, on first reading, awakened in me but little enthusiasm.

Conversely, I would say to the novice, "Beware lest an instant response to 'brilliance' leads you astray. Every play demands sober reflection before a final verdict is given."

While reading, the producer must absorb himself in the atmosphere not only of the period but also of the house, its inhabitants, the "emotional colour" of the play, its "shape," and its purport. He must ask himself innumerable questions about "what the author is driving at" and strive to give himself sound, convincing answers. Then, to employ the "orchestra" analogy, the producer must decide the "key" in which the play is written and the "over-all character" of the composition. Matters such as *tempo*, climax, and so on present themselves with the "stage" approach. Not yet will the producer have concerned himself very much with individual characters other than, perhaps, the leading protagonists—at least, not consciously.

Now on fairly intimate terms with his absent author, the producer relaxes mentally and allows the play to "take hold" of him. During this process he will invariably find unexpected light breaking in on some darkened places.

Next the play is studied from the "theatre angle." As he reads, the producer, more or less consciously, visualizes the play *in production*—he even "hears" the characters speaking and "sees" them in action. (This is still before casting). Obscurities diminish, but he need not worry greatly if a few remain.

The play now presents itself as a piece of dramatic literature, an example (irrespective of faults) of stage-craft, seen in perspective and awaiting the interpretive mind. Some written notes should be made, for the time is approaching when the producer must prepare his script—a process dealt with in Chapter III. First, however, he must be quite decided about all the major (and some of the minor) elements of interpretation, and matters of balance between scene and scene, between character and character. Problems will arise, both mechanical and personal. For the moment, the latter are the more important, for the play must now be cast. In all this, complete sincerity, artistic integrity, and inflexible fidelity to your author, so far as you have understood him, are essential.

Contrary to the apparent belief of some of our ultra-modern producers, it is neither their nor their actors' business to "re-write," in a production or an acting sense, any author's play. Capable dramatists who write with their tongues in their cheeks are, on the whole, rare. The majority are skilled writers, and many have a sound working knowledge of stagecraft. Both producer and actor may succeed in enriching a playwright's work, but they are only creative artists in the sense that they transmute the written word into human action and speech and set them in an acceptable visible frame that contributes to the author's purpose.

It *is* the producer's business to be correct in his estimation of "key" and "characterization" because these will, above all, influence his "treatment," both mechanical and emotional. This does not mean that some genuine misconceptions must of necessity destroy the play, provided they are not fundamental.

It is not, however, helpful to play a straight comedy as a somewhat artificial comedy of manners or a satire; or a "light comedy" as an extravagant farce, or naturalistic drama as if it were the latest thing in experimental

"expressionism." The precise touch of farcical extrava-
gance, of artificiality, or of imaginative fantasy must be
estimated as nearly as possible. It is sometimes, but not
always, the author's fault that the producer blunders.
The fundamentals having been decided, that very
important duty to the author must be faced—

Casting

The position of the producer on the casting committee can be, and frequently is, difficult. Some
producers (the cowards!) refuse to serve on it, and
reserve their complaints until later. How foolish to
court disaster in this way! He knows what he needs,
and the best possible casting is half-way towards
getting it. Moreover, in the amateur theatre there is
far more embarrassment caused by re-casting when
rehearsals have started than by refusal to agree on
certain castings while in committee. The captain of
the ship must share in the responsibility of engaging the
crew!

The best method, undoubtedly, is by audition before
a small committee of which the producer is a member.
The auditions should be followed by a general playreading of the provisional cast, before final decisions are
made. I have always found it most valuable to impress
on the cast that they are still provisional until the first
few rehearsals have taken place. This avoids some of
the "hard feelings" should it prove that the committee
have erred in judgment.

At the auditions, each candidate should be interviewed
in camera. The committee is dealing with amateurs
who frequently cannot do themselves justice in the
presence of even friendly rivals! The "I-know-I-shall-

be-dreadful-if-that-Jones-woman-is-in-the-room" state of mind is often excusable. In any event, privacy is the fairest method. The best way of getting a true estimate of an actor's suitability is to treat him on this occasion with sympathy, understanding, and encouragement—while tactfully checking any tendency to over-confidence.

Each candidate should have had a copy of the play and ample time to study it. Intelligent sight-reading is not a common accomplishment. I have been present at many "readings" where expensively educated people have been sadly incapable of expressive reading and have displayed barely a nodding acquaintance with vocal punctuation—an argument in favour of more and more play readings!

In any event, both amateurs and professionals are usually at their worst during an audition. If you and/or the committee "see" the candidate in the part but his audition is disappointing, discuss the character briefly with him and allow him to re-read the scene, or some other passage in which he may do himself more justice. Conversely, you will be surprised at times how an actor whom it has not occurred to you would be ideal in a certain character will show up well at an audition. You must not set too much store on this, but it does call for serious comparison with the favourite you have, perhaps, already backed.

There is one inflexible attitude the producer must adopt in casting; he must not be moved by any personal or private matters. Neither social standing, private relationship, ticket-selling capacity, nor any other non-artistic factor must ever concern him. The suitability of an artist in a given part is the producer's sole consideration. The ultimate responsibility is his, and the committee must provide the human material nearest to his ideal. In the amateur theatre, occasional limited compromise is inevitable. At the same time, the producer, though he will get the credit if proved right, must also be prepared to take the rap if proved wrong. But he cannot be expected to bear full responsibility if his artistic convictions are over-ruled.

Physical Appearance or Acting Ability?

Manifestly, the ideal is the actor who "looks the part" and who also has the right conception and acting ability. But, in an amateur production, there is rarely an unlimited choice.

The author sees HUBERT as "a tall, fair young man of military bearing, with a firm chin and keen blue eyes." You can hardly give that part to George, who is forty, under medium height, "a little thin on top," and displays the early signs of "middle-aged spread." Decision must be made on how much of the description is essential to the play. Probably "young" and "military bearing" are the two vital factors, but with these must be considered the appearance of the actor or actress most associated with him. Apart from these, intelligent interpretation is everything.

JULIE is "a pretty little thing, with dark brown curls, sympathetic eyes, and a ready, kindly smile that lights up her face with eagerness and vivacity." Obviously, the actress must not be very tall and gaunt, nor exceptionally buxom. It will not matter if she is blonde. If, however, she has a "hard" face, she will possibly possess too cold a nature and a "hard" attitude to life. Will she understand and sympathize with JULIE? Will she, irrespective of her technical skill, succeed in projecting the author's conception? These two questions demand decisive answers. One may feel in this instance that JULIE's *nature* is far more important than her *appearance*, although some approximation to the latter will assist the audience in "seeing" the character through the author's eyes. In this department of casting, compromise is more possible than in any other.

"Conception" or "Skill"?

The producer must, after compromise on "physical appearance," weigh the relative values of "imaginative conception" as against "technical skill." These two qualities do not always march together! I have, on countless occasions, been faced with an actor or actress of considerable training and experience yet lamentably lacking in ability to visualize the character or conceive the nature and degree of the emotions through which he or she must pass during the traffic of the play. Tough experience has shown me that in the majority of such cases I would far rather teach everything technical to a novice who has "conception" (and enthusiasm) than rehearse a skilled artist to whom the character is a completely intellectual and spiritual stranger. The work may be harder in one sense but invariably more rewarding!

"Personality Value" and "Balance"

Acting is a mutual, or *reciprocal*, function. We do not (or should not!) act in hermetically-sealed compartments. It follows, therefore, that in casting, considerable attention must be paid to this. The point is not only "Is Gerald the ideal SIR HENRY?" but also "Is

Gerald the ideal SIR HENRY *when playing opposite Edna as* HARRIET?"—and vice versa. Men and women all have their own "weight" of personality, both as individuals and as artists. The producer must gauge the precise degree of domination of one character over another so that balance is not destroyed. In the same way, he will judge how far *in individual scenes* one character dominates at one time and another at another. This is quite distinct from how the various scenes are played so that "story balance" is preserved.

Personality value and balance are bound up with considerations of appearance and physique that cannot be ignored. Normally, a hen-pecked husband will be visualized as much smaller than the domineering wife. Heavy personality is popularly associated with heavy physique! Yet it may well be that the author's fun derives largely from a tiny woman "crushing" a great lumbering spouse!

How true it is that the conductor must know his composer, his score—and his orchestra, too.

CHAPTER III

THE PRODUCER AND HIS SCRIPT

YOU have studied your play, and you understand it. You have cast it as satisfactorily as possible. There is, however, much to do before the first "reading rehearsal" is held.

Probably, you have an "acting edition" of the play, i.e., the play with "stage directions" introduced at appropriate places, a ground plan, perhaps an illustration of the original "settings," a list of the required furniture and properties, and even a "lighting plot." On the other hand, you may have a copy of the play with only the slightest indications of setting and action. You may even possess little more than a typescript of the dialogue.

However sparsely or fully your "script" is annotated, it will require careful preparation.

"Acting Editions"

Are "acting editions" good or bad? Every producer must be his own judge. There are acting editions— and acting editions! Some are detailed, accurate, and invaluable to the tyro-producer. Some are "fairly competent," and others are disastrous in their inaccuracy and ambiguity. Only experience will teach you how. far any edition is dependable. Let us leave it at that.

So far as the setting is concerned, you must take advantage of any information in the edition that is appropriate to the theatre, or hall, and the stage at your disposal. A great deal of what must be rejected for material reasons can, however, suggest possible improvisations. You will not be expected (it would be foolish to make the attempt) to reproduce on the stage of a parish hall (proscenium opening 20 ft., with a working depth of 14 ft.) everything in a photograph of the setting at the St. James's Theatre, London. Moreover, it is unnecessary to do so if you can faithfully suggest the setting, or the vital parts of it, and convey the general character and atmosphere of the play. The producer's business is to decide what is vital and what is not.

Again, the structure of the theatre and its stage may make it impossible to have the entrances exactly as in the original. For instance, the back wall of the "set" may be too near the permanent wall of the stage to permit a door in the back wall of the "room." It will, therefore, have to be up-stage in the R or L wall, and it may be helpful if this doorway is set in a short piece of angled wall. This provides for more effective entrances and exits by the characters, and off-stage space to show the "backing" beyond the door. Similar considerations may apply to other doors and windows. A producer must be able to improvise and to adapt to all working conditions.

Some furniture will be omitted, and much of it will be of a reduced size. Care should be exercised to retain the character of the pieces, even if their proportions must be varied.

The Ground Plan

This must be drawn to scale. It should be large, for the benefit of the stage staff. A large plan ready

to hand makes easier the "marking up" of the script.
Smaller replicas can be drawn later, one to slip into your
own copy of the play and another into that of your stage
manager, who will be an ever-present shadow at
rehearsals. The scale should be at least $\frac{1}{2}$ in. to the
foot. If the stage is small, the scale can be larger, say
$\frac{3}{4}$ in. to the foot.

In constructing the ground plan, the first consideration must be the problem of "the lines of sight." It
is useless to plan a setting and then to discover that
members of the audience in the side seats cannot see
some of the important action. Remember, too, that it
is within the precise limits of the stage setting that the
company must always rehearse.

In the theatre or hall will be taken the precise measurements of the stage, the "proscenium opening"—i.e.,
the width between the uprights of the proscenium arch,
allowing for the possible intrusion of the curtain
("house tabs"), which cannot always be drawn back
out of sight. The depth from the "setting line" (an
imaginary line across the stage between the down-
stage edges of the scenery on either side) to the back
wall of the stage should also be estimated. This
measurement does not represent the full "working
depth," for allowance must be made for space in which
the characters may cross the stage behind the scenery,
or the distance necessary between a stage window and
the back-cloth or backing depicting the distance scene,
or any essential space required for a door in the back
wall of the "set," beyond which there will be a piece
of "interior backing" to represent the "other room,"
a corridor, or a porch.

Next should be ascertained, by tactful and careful

inquiry, just where the front row of seats will be placed; how far the row will be from the edge of the proscenium arch, precisely where the extreme-end seats or chairs will be set, and the width of the side aisles. If there is a balcony at the back of the hall, it will be useful to know its height and distance, and also the height of the proscenium above stage level. In some productions, certain action could be obscured from the audience in the back of the balcony, but this question does not arise if the proscenium is reasonably high in relation to the balcony.

From these data should be drawn a plan similar to the illustration (Fig. 1). This shows a hall where the "line of sight" is a comparatively simple problem.

Note that the thin double lines represent the permanent walls. The heavy lines show the "scenery flats." The "broken" lines, drawn from the centres of the extreme seats, Row A. Nos. 1 and 16, to the corners of the proscenium arch and thence to the back of the scene, show the limits of vision for the occupants of these seats. They will be the greatest, but not the only, sufferers.

It is clear that a character "A," standing on the hearth-rug L with his back to the fire will be just seen. A character "B" entering R, will be seen an instant later, and almost to the last moment of his exit. Almost the entire setting will be within the visual range of every member of the audience with the exception of those who occupy A 1 and A 16, who, however, will only suffer the loss of what is contained between the lines of sight and the side flats, in which slender areas no important action that MUST be seen by all should be allowed to take place.

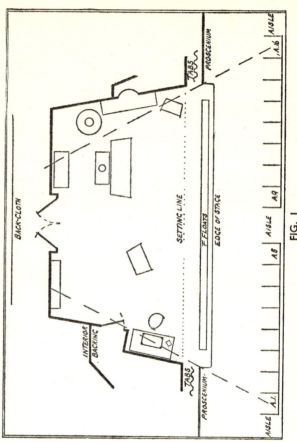

FIG. 1

In Fig. 1, the door R has been set "in-stage" a little by a "return," probably about 18 ins. deep, and both side-walls are set at a slight angle. It might be suggested that the walls could have been set at right angles with the "floats" and that the door R could have been down-stage, below the desk. True, but there are some reasons against this course. Adoption of this suggestion could result in an appreciable proportion of the audience losing important features of the side-walls, and the characters playing with their backs to the fire would be excessively "profiled." Moreover, down-stage is a bad place for a leading character to make an important entrance. Players enter thus at a "non-dominant" spot, and almost immediately have to travel in a somewhat UP-stage direction. This nearly always robs such an entrance of some effectiveness.

Imagine a situation in which the setting is as in Fig. 1.

The only occupant of the stage is SIR HENRY, a cold, unemotional man, who is seated at the desk, R, writing. HARRIET, who is a little afraid of him, enters R. She is almost immediately visible, and registers a reaction on finding him there:

HARRIET   (*reacting*). Oh—there you are, Henry.
SIR HENRY (*without turning*; *coldly*). Yes.
             (HARRIET *closes the door quietly.*)
    (*Writing.*) I wish to speak to you.
HARRIET   (*reacting*; *in a low voice*). Oh. (*She moves slowly towards the settee.*)

Note that (*a*) SIR HENRY can be far more "crushing" by not looking up or turning to her; (*b*) HARRIET faces the house to get her reactions "over"; (*c*) no major movement is required until this "moment" has been fully registered and the "atmosphere" established.

In the setting Fig. 2, however, HARRIET, on entrance, has to react and say her line turned slightly UP-stage, and SIR HENRY's "Yes" must be said while they are, in

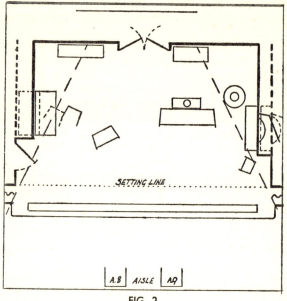

FIG. 2

a sense, facing each other, even if he does not look *up*. Then HARRIET has to "break the moment" by crossing towards C, until SIR HENRY can give his second phrase with his back to her, by which time he will not be so intensely "crushing" as he would have been with Fig. 1. Certainly the majority of entrances under Fig. 2. will

lose throughout the play, since the door is DOWN-stage.
The above incident would be even worse if the R wall
were not set IN-stage (as the dotted lines show) and
the effect of not IN-staging the L wall is also manifest.
If the stage is, on the other hand, small, this in-staging
causes great restriction of movement.

Drawing in the Setting

This is constructed with the setting line as a base.
Walls, window, fire, and door having been drawn, fill
in the furniture—as much of the original as can be
accommodated and is vital. This also must be drawn
to scale as nearly as possible, at first lightly in pencil,
because as the script is worked through it may be
necessary to adjust the positions of the pieces in order
to get effective groupings on a smaller stage, and
sufficient space for crossings and other movements by
the characters. During this process much will be done
by "trial and error," but eventually the best setting to
cover all the important "pictures" and moves that the
play demands will be decided.

Marking Positions, Movements, and Groups

A clear idea of positions, broad movements, and the
more important dramatic groupings should be formed
before entering the rehearsal room. Adjustments must
be left to early rehearsals, and decisions on minor
details must not be too rigid until then. Nothing
convinces a cast of a producer's incompetence more
than when he has to work out major movements (with
inevitable changes of mind in the process!) during
rehearsal.

Fig. 3 indicates the "acting areas" of a stage. The
2

divisions drawn are arbitrary; for example, an actor may be regarded as "at RC" although he is no more than on the R edge of the C division. Again, an actor may be said to "move down to L C" without necessarily occupying the square thus designated. In this instance, the expression would mean that the player had to move DOWN-stage from an UP-stage position and

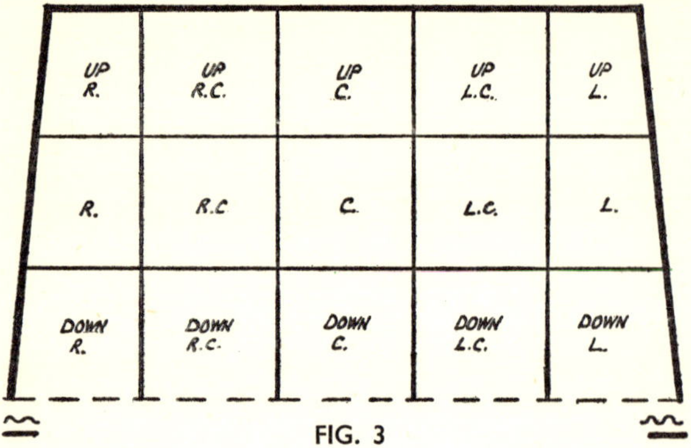

UP R.	UP R.C.	UP C.	UP L.C.	UP L.
R.	R.C	C.	L.C.	L.
DOWN R.	DOWN R.C.	DOWN C.	DOWN L.C.	DOWN L.

FIG. 3

was then "left of centre" without having reached the extreme L zone.

Great imagination should be exercised and cultivated during the process of "marking up," for every moment of the play. You will find it rather like a game of chess; constantly having to think one or even several moves ahead. For instance, you will have designed what appears to be a most effective "picture"—only to find, a page or so later, that you have not allowed for a quick, clean, even breath-taking exit for EDNA, some essential business for GEORGE, or a shattering entrance for HUBERT—none of which will be possible with the grouping you have devised. For instance, in Fig. 4, EDNA and JOHN are in violent conflict. They have a relatively UP-stage position, and the witnesses to this altercation are suitably grouped. But—the incident terminates with a whirlwind exit of EDNA *down L*, She has a large armchair at C, and a closely-knit trio

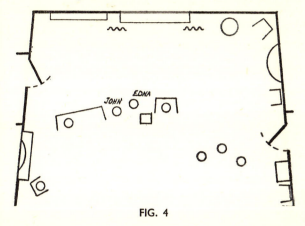

FIG. 4

down L C, barring her way. An instantaneous break-up of this trio is unthinkable, and the play demands that the picture is "held" until after her exit.

Fig. 5 shows the correct grouping. You will have to retrace your steps and now arrange that the "trio" is at R, and EDNA and JOHN are at L C. It will probably be permissible for JOHN to "ease up" level with EDNA just before her exit-cross, or she may be able to brush him aside (a little up and to L) to give herself a clean cross. She will, by the way, probably divide her last line, using the final phrase as an "exit line" as she goes

out.   There is, however, no hard and fast rule for this.
Everything depends on the character, the line, and the
purport of the scene.   This principle is applied to every
instance of "manœuvring" characters. If GEORGE
must quickly and most unexpectedly produce a document or revolver from a bureau, he must be cunningly
manœuvred into position in time, neither too early nor

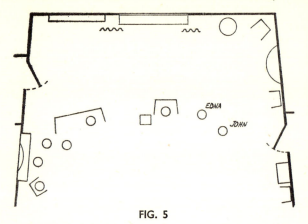

FIG. 5

unconvincingly "just in time"! You will find it an
intricate business that demands imagination, thought,
and patience.   Yet how fascinating it proves to be!
    Whether you are a beginner or not, do not despise the
stage directions supplied. If the entrances and the
arrangement of the furniture do not vary drastically
from the original, these directions will be helpful.   Ask
yourself constantly WHY they have been so devised; you
will invariably find that although they appear to concern the mechanics of acting they are also of great

emotional significance. For instance, "dramatic domination" is influenced largely by position on the stage. Broadly, a character cannot dominate another, or a group, from a DOWN-stage position. If he is down-stage near C he has nothing to address but the floats! If down R or down L, he must "play up-stage" or partly profiled, which, again, robs him of domination, unless, perhaps, he is perched on a rostrum, a low stair-case, or on some structure that raises him above stage level. Even then, this position is rarely of maximum effectiveness. Styles of acting and production vary with the character of the play, but this fundamental truth remains, that the most dominant position for any character at any moment is UP C, or UP-stage near C, with the subordinate characters DOWN-stage in relation to himself. The tyrannical father, the commanding officer, the dictator, the criminal with the revolver, the revengeful woman facing her victims—for all of these, *that* must be the relative position when the moment of domination or threat is reached. While marking the script in preparation, these broad principles must be applied.

Stage Directions

Stage directions are of two kinds. There are the "mechanical" directions that concern those things just discussed, and there are those that may be regarded purely as "emotional" directions. These concern "how a line is spoken" and details of action and re-action to portray feeling. They are often valuable indications of the effect the author wishes to convey, but they must not be accepted as dogmatic instructions on the means to be employed. We act from the inside, outwards; our portrayal is through the medium of the actor's personality—harnessed to his craftsmanship. The actor visualizes the part in the light of his conception of the author's intention, but "A" will project that idea (or attempt to do so) by a somewhat different method from that employed by "B." "A," in co-operation with his producer, will decide that a line is more—or less—intense, or satirical, or tender than "B" and *his* producer, and so on. This is more fully discussed in Chapters V and VI.

Many of these "emotional stage directions" are legitimate, and cannot be ignored. Such suggestions as "gently," "coldly," "ironically," and "gaily," are quite in order and—all too frequently!—necessary. Even "looking down shyly" and "clenching his fists" are hints that can be accepted in many cases. When, however, an author goes into detail and insists on a character "snarling through his teeth," "tearing his hair and waving his arms wildly," and other shades of facial expression and gesture, I think the actor is justified in asking himself whether he is to *act* or turn himself into a marionette! Mr. "X" will register admirably by doing just what the author says (in moderation!) while Mr. "Y" will, on the other hand, give a superb performance by doing nothing of the kind.

Since, however, as a producer of amateurs, you will have to give instruction in the craft of acting, your own ideas should be noted on your script but left fairly "open" until you see of what the actors are capable imaginatively and in projection.

Points on "suspense," "climax," "pause," and changes of *tempo* should also be included tentatively. A few small but accurate sketches—ground plans in miniature—should be made, and inserted in your copy at the appropriate pages in order to show what the grouping is to be at given points in the play. Do not regard the script as "marked" until everything has been considered a second, or even a third, time.

CHAPTER IV

THE PRODUCER AND HIS STAFF

THE captain of the ship performs his duties chiefly on the bridge and in the chart room. He makes no attempt to stoke, lubricate, or control the engines, to cook the meals in the galley, to dispatch radio messages, or to organize deck sports. His responsibility is to see that the ship reaches the correct port, safely and on time.

The play producer, similarly, does not make the scenery, obtain furniture, lights and props, control the switchboard, raise and lower the "tabs," or sell programmes.

The essence of good organization is not doing things but getting things done—by other people. There is a good deal of truth in this saying.

On the other hand, neither the post of producer nor of captain is a sinecure. Yet both are dependent for success on an adequate, competent, and loyal staff.

Although some reduction may be made safely if the show is not "heavy" as to scenery or complicated in other respects, the full personnel for the producer of an amateur company is:

> STAGE DIRECTOR
> STAGE MANAGER
> ASSISTANT STAGE MANAGERS (1 or 2)
> ELECTRICIAN
> ASSISTANT ELECTRICIAN
> PROPERTY MASTER
> WARDROBE MISTRESS

In addition there are such stage hands as the production requires for scene-shifting and similar duties.

The functions of each member of the staff may be described thus:

The STAGE DIRECTOR is, in effect, the deputy-producer, who will always take rehearsals should the producer be unavoidably absent. He will usually rehearse understudies. He is the closest associate of the producer, and acts as liaison officer between him and the rest of the staff. If the company is small and the production relatively simple (particularly if the theatre is not large), his office can be merged into that of the—STAGE MANAGER, the S.M., in whom is vested considerable authority. He confers with and receives from the producer and stage director the schedules ("plots") of all the material and mechanical requirements for the production. These are: scenery; furniture; properties; sound and other "effects."

The lighting plot is not included in these, for this goes (perhaps via the stage director) direct from the producer to the electrician.

The S.M. and his assistants (under the S.D. if such an official is appointed) are responsible for receiving hired scenery and its "setting up."

If the company makes and paints its own scenery, the S.M. has the similar duties of ensuring that it is right in dimensions, design and *décor*.

The stage director and/or the S.M., are directly responsible to the producer for securing by hire or loan all the furniture, hangings, pictures, and stage props. These are submitted to the producer for approval before final arrangements are made.

The stage director and/or the S.M. are provided

2*

with marked copies of the play. He, or one of his assistants, must be present at and watch *every* rehearsal. Any revisions or adjustments of positions, movements, or "business" made in rehearsal are inserted in the copy at the time. This saves argument on future occasions, and thus a "prompt copy" is prepared as rehearsals proceed.

During the rehearsal period, the S.M. must bring to the notice of the stage director or the producer any problems arising out of the provision of the items set out in the "plots," for nothing must be left until the eleventh hour. Periodic conferences to report progress are advisable.

At all stage and dress rehearsals, and at all performances, the S.D. or the S.M. has full control of the stage area and everything that happens in his department. He also has considerable authority over the players. If their presence "on stage" (whether the curtain be up or down) interferes with smooth working, he can dismiss them to their dressing-rooms. He will also enforce the NO TALKING and NO SMOKING orders, both of which should have been made crystal-clear to the cast beforehand.

The stage director and/or the stage manager with their staff set the stage and furniture before each act. The producer is not expected to be present, having duties elsewhere (See Chapter X) until the stage is ready to be "passed."

ASSISTANT STAGE MANAGER. For a three-act production, two "A.S.M's" are advisable. Their duties are primarily concerned with those of the S.M., whose subordinates they are. When the ordinary stage hands have set the scenery, with or without the assistance of the S.M. and the A.S.M's, the latter help to set and to adjust the furniture, hangings, etc. The A.S.M's will also be responsible for "stage props" such as crockery, cutlery, and food for meals, the revolver in the desk, the telegram on the mantel-shelf, and the incriminating document in the Chinese vase! It is not unusual, if these duties do not prove too onerous, to add to them by making one A.S.M. the prompter and the other the call-boy. The former should have attended several rehearsals and, indeed, officiated as "prompt" thereat in order that he or she may be familiar with the text and know where "pauses" occur and the duration of each. The call-boy A.S.M. will rehearse himself at the final rehearsals. His function is to knock at all dressing-room doors and to call "Half-hour, please." This is repeated for "Quarter of an hour" and also "Beginners, please," five minutes before the beginning of the over-ture music. The call-boy should also call all players during performance some minutes before they are due to make each entrance, unless they have observed that the player is already waiting in the wings. The call-boy (or one of the A.S.M's) should also be made responsible for checking "personal" or "hand" props with each player. For this purpose the A.S.M. is supplied with a "Personal Property Plot." A section of it will read something like this:

ACT 1.

SIR HENRY	Cigarette case, filled. Lighter.
	(*2nd entrance.*) Telegram.
	(*3rd entrance.*) Broken porcelain statuette.
HARRIET	Handbag containing compact, handker-chief, and diary. Pencil.

(*2nd entrance.*) Letter—blue paper—
opened. No handbag.
(*4th entrance.*) Small green bottle. Bandage
on "cut" finger.

Many amateur players are just as reliable over
personal props as any professional; the ultimate responsibility must be theirs. It does no harm, however, to
have a check, especially in an exceptionally exciting
and complicated play, or one with frequent exits and
re-entrances.

The PROPERTY MASTER is one whose duties are sometimes merged into that of the S.M., who not infre-
quently has a gift for making unusual "props." Parch-
ment documents impressively sealed, Renaissance
goblets, blood-stained daggers, spinning-wheels, and
Chinese idols joyfully occupy his long winter evenings,
and who can produce the ancestral portrait more
mysteriously, yet convincingly, than he? Sometimes
he manifests himself as the *alter ego* of the stage carpenter.
Sometimes, alas, he does not exist at all, and his miracles
must be the product of communal effort.

The WARDROBE MISTRESS and her own staff function
only when a "costume play" is in hand. She confers
directly with the producer, and together they bring out
a costume plot, in which style, colour, and other details
are included. The wardrobe mistress superintends the
measurement-taking of each actor or actress, including
wig measurements, and fills up the charts usually supplied by the theatrical costumiers for this purpose.
When the "wardrobe" is received, the wardrobe
mistress and assistants unpack, check, and hand out the
costumes. These are tried on and paraded, after which

the wardrobe staff are responsible for the return and exchange of costumes that are wrong, for minor alterations, and for repairs during the run of the play. Finally, they are responsible for the return of the costumes in good order to the hiring firm.

The STAGE ELECTRICIAN usually works directly with the producer during the preparatory stages, the S.D. co-operating. The electrician is a technician in electrical matters, and by experience becomes a useful adviser on how various effects and "atmospheres" are secured in terms of light. On the other hand, although the producer may not know an "ohm" from an "amp" or a "watt" from a "volt," he must acquire a working knowledge of stage lighting equipment, types of lamps, and the purpose of each; colour media, how to mix and control these; the intensities and angles of direction of light beams for the achievement of the desired results.

The initial co-operation with the producer must be a discussion of how far the available lighting equipment will provide for the lighting cues in the plot, and to what extent additional equipment should be hired, if this is permissible. The electrician may be in a position to suggest methods whereby reasonable results may be obtained with the existing installation. Since this is not a textbook on stage lighting, technical details are not discussed here. They are dealt with specially in another volume in this Series. It should be stressed, however, that the lighting plot should be clearly expressed; also that the stage electrician is master on the switchboard, as the S.D. or S.M. is on the stage.

The wise producer will call a conference, or series of

conferences, with all his staff, before rehearsals begin. When all are fully briefed, he should leave them to their individual jobs (except for progress reports), for now he is to meet his cast, formally and in force, for the first time.

CHAPTER V

THE PRODUCER AND HIS CAST

THERE is no form of activity in which cordial personal relationships, mutual understanding, and a "happy atmosphere" are more necessary than in play production. The creation and maintenance of these depend greatly, though not wholly, on the producer. He need not possess all the virtues and nobilities of character, and no human failings. At the same time, he must steer successfully between the Scylla of dictatorship and the Charybdis of excessive "easy good-fellowship."

It is wise to make it clear from the first that, without any ill-feeling, there must be no "nonsense." At the same time, the producer must never allow any member of cast (or staff) to feel afraid to approach him, nor must he ever withhold genuine sympathy and advice.

He will soon find, on the other hand, that there are a few types (not confined only to the amateur stage) of which he must beware, and with which he must be firm from the beginning. Here are some examples, none of them imagined. All have been encountered by every producer:

(1) The actor (and actress) who delivers himself (or herself) thus: "Of course, Mr. X, you understand that I never even begin to give a performance until the last week of rehearsal—I *mean*, I never give a *thing* until then." Fantastic? No—surprisingly common. These

precious creatures really believe that this attitude is a proof of genius. They choose to forget—or are unaware—that our great actors have, substantially, the opposite approach. Where would a company be, I wonder, if they did not know until the last few days how Mr. Alec Guinness and Miss Edith Evans proposed to play their parts? As the character "grows on" the player it begins to flower, and his fellow players, observing the growth, develop their own portrayals in harmony, even if there be conflict and adjustment *en route*. This is what is meant by true reciprocal acting. Let there be no mistake; this kind of player must change his or her attitude at once, or the part must be re-cast immediately.

(2) The player who will *not* "take production." He or she will soon be known. It will be obvious tacit rebellion, not inability. The danger here is twofold. First, this subtle form of mutiny spreads infection. Moreover, if it is not dealt with, you are faced with a worse danger, namely, that the player will, eventually, yield, play as required in rehearsal, and then deliberately betray you and the members of the cast by reverting to his or her own rendering when the curtain has risen on the public performance. Such a thing sounds as incredible as my first example, but I have met this individual too often to have any illusions on the subject. This type of player demands firm, nay, relentless treatment. There must be an early understanding and an honourable pledge. If ultimate treachery follows, the player must never be permitted to play for that company again.

Then we have the cheerful "I'll be all right on the night-er," the unpunctual, the habitual absentee, the

player who wants to debate with you on every con-
ceivable point, and, perhaps, variants of these. But
perhaps I have given you sufficient advice on (1) and
(2) to cover most of your personal problems!

Acting Abilities

The producer must try to gauge the degree of acting
skill of each of his players as soon as he can. This will
assist him in estimating which scenes will need most
tuition in technique. Occasionally, he will find that a
novice will require less intensive rehearsal than experienced artistes because the conception of the former
happens to be more vivid than that of the latter. It is
not uncommon to find, moreover, that the beginner
adheres more faithfully to correct technique than do
some "old hands," who, in the course of time, have
slipped into bad acting-habits. Perhaps I should
apologize for the cliché, but there is such a thing as the
familiarity that breeds contempt!

Conferences and Readings

Before the first rehearsal, the producer will be well
advised to hold at least one "round-table conference"
with his cast, followed by a "reading" and one or two
subsequent readings.

The conference must be frank, and even the humblest
participant encouraged to express views and ideas. It
is necessary for the players to learn what is the producer's interpretation of the author's intention. It is no
less vital for the producer to discover what, up to this
time, have been the reactions of every member of the
cast to the study of the play. The resultant discussions
should establish in the minds of all the "key" of the

composition, and also clear ideas of individual characterization.

Having achieved a reasonable measure of agreement, the members of the cast proceed to a reading of the play, being first enjoined to keep in mind, as they read, the fundamentals on which they are in accord.

During the first reading, the producer should try not to interrupt. He must listen intently and make written notes. The reading over, he deals with the points noted, stresses misconceptions, and reminds the cast of forgotten matters. Now the cast reads the play again, endeavouring to express the author's intention as fully as it is possible at this stage. There may not be time to hold two readings of the whole play at one session, especially following the conference. It will in this case be more advantageous to do Act 1 twice, than Act 1 and Act 2 once each.

These readings will be almost valueless if the players use ordinary conversational tones as if they are reading to each other in strict privacy! The producer *must* insist on the cast "pitching" their voices exactly as if they were on the stage with an audience present. This is not to be construed as an order to shout, nor does it entail the least vocal strain. If the voice is employed correctly, there is no more physical fatigue in "throwing" it than in indulging in the confidential mumblings so beloved by some professionals both in London and the Provinces.

Incidentally, I would stress that this inflexible rule about "pitching" the voice as if on the stage of a theatre applies equally to every rehearsal, from beginning to end. How ridiculous it is for a player to imagine that he or she can characterize and portray any kind of emotion, whether it be in farce, comedy, or tragedy, in a private and confidential voice. He is in worse trouble when he suddenly awakens to the knowledge that he is about to face several hundred people in a theatre and must suddenly begin to use an altogether different voice in order to be audible! On the other hand, if he has pitched his voice from the beginning, he continues thus when the public performances open, apart from any slight vocal adjustment that he finds later is demanded by the acoustics of the particular theatre.

Whenever I have encountered inaudibility at a drama festival I have invariably discovered that this rule has not been adopted.

"Tempo" and "Climax"

Little can be said to the cast on these points until rehearsals begin. It will be useful at the conference, however, to give general indications of major variations in *tempo*, and to stimulate imagination by discussing the more exciting climactic "moments."

The principal objects of the conference and preliminary readings should now have been achieved—the establishment of mutual understanding, the frank exchange of views, a homogeneity of approach, and a general unanimity of conception of the author's intention.

CHAPTER VI

INTERPRETATION AND TREATMENT

BEFORE we enter the rehearsal room for the first time, let us discuss plays in general, their interpretation, and varying forms of "treatment."

The importance of placing the play in the right category—farce, light comedy, satirical comedy, domestic drama and so on has already been stressed. At the same time, study of the script has enabled us to estimate the "key" of the composition. What do we really mean by "key"? Most plays contain both "dramatic" and "comedy" elements, often sharply contrasted. Does this mean that some parts of the play are in one "key" and others in another? No. A play is like a symphony composed in one key, and yet possesses variations of mood, which are expressed by variations of treatment. The "key" of the play refers more to its general or "over-all" purport. That is to say, the author intends, in satire, to be lightly, wittily, even flippantly satirical, or bitterly, even searingly so. In other words, his play may be sheer entertainment— or a cautery. A comedy or a drama may be a sincere commentary on life and human nature, or it may depart from realism for "escapist" entertainment purposes, or in the direction of experimental "expressionism" or some form of fantasy to suit the author's special purpose. The essential thing is that he must not mix his *styles*, his work must be homogeneous in order to carry conviction. *and* the actor's treatment must be equally consistent. The mixing of styles in one play is frequently misunderstood. How is it, one may ask, that Sean O'Casey in, say, *The Plough and The Stars*, can switch us instantaneously from irrepressible laughter to terror and tears? Is this not mixing oil and water, or, to revert to the musical analogy, a change of "key"? The answer is, again, "No," for in all the scenes, regardless of *the nature of the emotion aroused*, the *degree* of "realism" is the same. Indeed, in most of his plays O'Casey succeeds in swinging from tragedy to something *akin* to farce and back, and to and fro, again and again, without the least danger of "losing" his audience—always providing the acting is right. At the zenith of his success, his most criticized (and, perhaps his least convincing) play was *The Silver Tassie* in which he alternated between bitter realism and "expressionism." Whether the various forms of experimental drama appeal to one or not is immaterial. The point is that here we have an almost classic instance of the failure of a great playwright to "change key" within the fabric of his play.

Treatment Control

The producer of comedy will find that his most common problem will be the tendency of his players to tip over the edge into the realm of farce. This arises mostly from a natural anxiety to "get laughs." In light comedy, the writer, too, is faced with the constant temptation to exaggerate the fun. His responsibility is to decide whether he is going to write a comedy or a farce—and to stick to his decision! Characters have a way of "running away" from their authors, so this problem is not so easy to solve as it sounds. When this has occurred, the producer and player must combine in restoring a unanimity of treatment so far as this is possible. Similar situations will face them in "dramatic" plays. The precise quality and degree of "naturalism" must be gauged and adhered to strictly. "Melodrama" in the old sense of the term does not often make its appearance to-day—except to be burlesqued. But in "thrillers" or other forms of "escapist drama," a certain departure from realism (strictly controlled) is permissible.

"Naturalism"

It is necessary to be quite clear from the start exactly what is meant by this term. It is applied to the treatment of every type of play which (whether drama or comedy) is intended to be a realistic reflection of, or commentary on, life as we see it.

This is not a textbook on the technique of acting, which is analysed in another volume in this Series. It is, however, worth pointing out here that in the sphere of "realism" it is not the player's business to "be" natural. But it most certainly *is* the player's function to *create the illusion of nature,* a different and far more complex task—and it provides the reason why "technique" is required!

Acting is, indeed, the art that conceals art; the whole business of acting is the creation of illusion. From the first moment, when the curtain rises, the audience must be transported to another, yet "real," world, and must only be subconsciously aware that they are in a theatre and that it is all "make-believe."

It is strange yet true that if the actor behaves *really*

naturally (i.e., as he does, or would do, in private life) he is immediately unconvincing as a "naturalist" actor. It is only when he is *acting* (within the true limits of technically artistic "naturalism") that he deceives his audience into thinking that he is "being natural." Any departure from this method must be not in the direction of "private" naturalism, but in that of the particular artistic treatment that the character and type of play demand.

The "Shape" of a Play

It is a generally accepted principle that in the majority of plays the first act is mainly "exposition," the second concerned with the development of the conflict (with the highest point of climax at the "curtain"), and the third with the resolution of the problem, or some other satisfactory form of termination. At the same time, the curve of interest and excitement is not uniform in every play. These may be imagined as graphs plotted like temperature charts, in which will be observed a marked difference between the patients! Moreover, the producer will note the balance between the intensity of comedy and the intensity of drama as between scene and scene. Reference must be made to it here since it plays an important part in gauging "shape." The producer, at periodic "runs through," must keep a sharp eye on the maintenance of shape and balance. It brings us, moreover, to an important discussion on:

How Emotional Effect is Produced

Almost anyone with a minimum of musical knowledge can stand up and beat three, or four, in a bar with a baton; but that is not *conducting*. It requires little skill to "hold a script," read out stage directions, and "prompt." That is not *producing*.

If you watch a fine conductor you will observe how at one moment he is suppressing the "brass," at another giving a "lead" to the "woodwind," urging his orchestra to a *crescendo* or an *accelerando*, soothing them to *piano* or *pianissimo*, or ensuring that a *rallentando* is not too soon, too late, or too marked.

This is where the "conductor" analogy is most applicable to the producer, for emotional effect both in individual and collective acting is achieved more by variation of *tempo*, and of tone, than, perhaps, any other means. There are no rigid rules, and dogmatism is dangerous. As a general principle, however, it will be found that excitement, fury, terror, increasing "fun," and farcical confusion are normally accompanied by a heightened *tempo*, a quickening of pace in speech and action. The doomful moments, passages of pathos, periods of philosophic exchange, comedy that derives from indolence, are examples of treatment that are marked by a relatively slow *tempo*. There will be exceptions in both categories. For instance, a "conspiratorial" incident in one play will need quick, sharp playing. The dialogue of this passage will probably be crisply written and "liney," that is to say, composed of brief speeches of only a few words each. In another play a conspiratorial passage will call for a relatively slow *tempo*, and there is a likelihood here that individual speeches will be more amply written than in the former example.

Another general principle is that the quicker and more exciting the scene the greater the volume of vocal tone.

For instance, we all speak more loudly when we are angry than when we are kind. We are all inclined to raise our voices when we are convulsed with laughter and to lower them when we are sad. Again, there will be exceptions. To employ the former example (of conspiracy), the pitch of voice will be governed chiefly by the likelihood, or otherwise, of the conspirators being overheard! The various changes in, and combinations of, pace and tone are matters, primarily, for the producer's direction.

Tempo—Real and Apparent

There is one fundamental truth about pace that every producer must learn himself and impart to all his players. It is this: there is a profound difference between *real time* and *stage time*. That is to say, a pause, or a piece of action unaccompanied by dialogue ("silent bus.") which occupies five or six seconds of actual time seems, to the *audience*, to have occupied anything from eight to twelve seconds, according to the prevailing mood, but certainly much more than the *real* time. It follows, therefore, that whatever illusion the player wishes to create, his pause, or "silent bus.," must occupy less *real* time than the apparent time. This is why cues must be "picked up" so quickly, and dialogue "stream-lined." A hesitation of less than one second seems like a second or more, and the general impression on the audience is that of lagging, disjointed conversation. The same principle must be applied to the pace of delivery of the dialogue itself, which does not mean an excuse, however, for "gabbling" or faulty articulation. Variations in *tempo* and tone, then, are primary factors in creating emotional effect or interpreting lines. There are also "vocal punctuation," the pause, correct distribution of emphasis, and physical action to be considered, but these will be dealt with in Chapter VII in which the successive stages of rehearsal method are treated.

There is, however, one last injunction on the *producer's* attitude towards the player's craft: Do not forget that there are two major and distinct elements in acting—the "conception" and the "projection." If you are to extract the maximum value from your author's work, you must impress this truth upon your cast. A comedian can paint his nose red and put on a comic hat—it does not make him funny. It makes him look funny—for a time. Sooner or later the attitude of the audience will be: "Well, come on, now make us laugh." And if the fun is not inside the comedian, ready to bubble out—he is lost!

So, too, in tragedy. The player must "have that within which passeth show," and not only "the trappings and the suits of woe." The first, imaginative element, is essential to the second, which is largely a matter of the physical mechanics of acting. This is not to say that the player suffers the emotion (either comic or tragic) in the moment of acting. His personal emotional experience occurs during the process of conception. It colours, but must not control, his actual work upon the stage.

CHAPTER VII

REHEARSAL METHOD—1. MECHANICS

NO producer should embark on rehearsals without having planned a schedule of the work that he intends to cover at each, and a copy of this must be sent to every player as soon as possible after the final meeting of the casting committee.

The schedule of rehearsals varies for every play. It is governed chiefly by the following considerations:

(1) Nature of play.
(2) Size of cast.
(3) Total duration of rehearsal period.
(4) Evenings when all the cast are available, and when some are not.
(5) Relative importance, or difficulty, of various scenes.
(6) Existence of "crowd" scenes, where "supers" and numbers of small part players are involved.
(7) Various local conditions and difficulties.

Obviously, when casting, the standpoint of the producer and the committee must be "the show comes first." At the same time, this consideration may make some concessions imperative. There may well be instances of casting so nearly ideal that withholding a limited degree of compromise about rehearsal nights would be the height of folly.

Unfortunately, amateur rehearsals of a straight play are frequently stretched over far too long a period. Operatic productions rarely exceed four weeks. A section of a rehearsal schedule should read something like this:

TEMPLETOWN THESPIANS

"THE MELTON MYSTERY"

SCHEDULE OF REHEARSALS

Date	Time	Place	Act	Remarks
Mon., 10th Jan.	7.15	St. Peter's Hall.	ALL in ACT 1. Positions, etc.	
Tues., 11th Jan.	7.15	St. Peter's Hall.	ALL in ACT 1.	
Thur., 13th Jan.	7.15	Corner Café.	PRINCIPALS in ACT 2, Sc. 1. Positions.	"BARKER," "GEORGE" and SUPERS not required.
Fri., 14th Jan.	7.15	St. Peter's Hall.	ALL in ACT 2. Sc. 1, Sc. 2. Positions, etc.	FULL ACT 2 Cast.
Mon., 17th Jan.	7.15	St. Peter's Hall.	ALL in ACT 3. Positions.	
Tues., 18th Jan.	7.15	St. Peter's Hall.	ALL in ACT 3.	
Thur., 20th Jan.	7.15	Corner Café.	ALL in ACT 2. Sc. 2 only.	*Note.*—"BARKER," "GEORGE," and SUPERS must attend.
Fri., 21st Jan.	7.15	St. Peter's Hall.	FULL CO. for ACT 1, ACT 2, Sc. 1, ACT 3.	ABOVE NOT REQUIRED.

Later sections will show entire evenings devoted to "special scenes," in which only a few players are involved, others where the entire cast are required on a date that may appear to be surprisingly early. These features will be due, respectively, to the need to conquer difficult scenes (i.e., difficult to interpret emotionally or involving complicated and detailed "business") and the value of periodic revisions or "runs through" to enable the whole company to keep the entire play in perspective and fresh.

The preparation of the rehearsal schedule demands considerable thought, since upon its perfect planning depends the "building up" of the production in stages of ideal sequence so that no section of the play is neglected while others become "stale" by over-rehearsal.

The First Rehearsal

In an amateur production the earliest rehearsals may be attended only by those of the cast who are concerned in the act under consideration. As soon as the play is well under way, however, the entire cast should be present, whenever possible, in order that everyone may get the "shape" of the play and adjust accurately their stage relationship to the characters with which they are associated and their individual "places" in the story.

The cast is assembled for the first rehearsal. Each member has his, or her, copy of the play *and a pencil*. Before their arrival, the S.M. and A.S.M. have marked out the limits of the scenery, perhaps with chalk lines, or with "walls" of chairs with which the rehearsal-hall may be provided. The exits are clearly indicated by gaps between chairs, and the furniture must be represented as nearly as possible by tables, chairs, and so on.

Either the S.M. or one of the A.S.M's will be in constant attendance on the producer and provided with a copy of the play and the ground plan. The cast will first gather around the producer, *facing the set*, with the ground plan before them, the scene is carefully described, and points of confusion are cleared up by question and answer.

As soon as the producer is confident that his players visualize the scene, they retire to seats conveniently near yet clear of the set, and are enjoined to watch and to keep reasonably quiet. Here it is as well to mention that incessant "giggle and chatter" is forbidden. On the other hand, a rehearsal-room is not a Trappist monastery. A moderate amount of more or less inaudible conversation (in the remotest corners of the room!) should distress only the most temperamental of producers. At the same time, the more the players are encouraged to listen and to watch (and thereby to *learn*), the less garrulous they will become—even the females! Much will depend upon how interesting the producer can make the rehearsal.

At the first rehearsal, the cast is occupied with Act I. The players are taken through their entrances, major movements, and exits, reading their dialogue in clear, well-pitched voices. The players make marginal notes of any revisions of movement, etc., differing from what is printed in the script. These notes must be made at the time, and the S.M. and the A.S.M. will also note them if they are adjustments of what the producer has already written in his "marked" script.

At present, the producer does not trouble his players with technical faults in acting, or deviations from the agreed basic characterization. As the rehearsal proceeds he will, so far as appears wise, deal with "major business," but usually in a first session the broad "positions and movements" of a single act should be mastered as thoroughly as possible, and no more.

I advocate strongly the completion of "positions and major business" of the entire play before any "interpretive" rehearsals are embarked upon. When these latter begin for each successive act, only a "re-cap." on positions should be necessary.

Another feature that always pays a dividend is the compression of the purely "mechanical" rehearsals into a period of nearly consecutive nights. Even if the interpretive rehearsals must be more "spread over" (though this must be avoided as far as possible) it does assist the cast to "get into" the play if the positions are mastered during an intensive and closely-knit series of rehearsals.

As the mechanics are conquered, the producer must begin to introduce elements of characterization. I remind the reader that, from the first session, the players have read their parts with well-pitched voices. This habit facilitates considerably their early attempts at characterization and, indeed, before long they interpret to some extent unconsciously, and the "theatre pitch" of their voices is almost "second nature" to them.

On the other hand, what the producer will have most in mind at this stage will be the perfection, or otherwise, of his marked script! He will discover (but must not be too dismayed) that it is one thing to visualize a group, a stage picture, or a series of movements in private, and to devise it on paper, and quite another when his players are endeavouring to reproduce his script in action. He may note some instances of "masking," a character here and there may not be in an ideal position for a verbal exchange with another, or, an entire picture may prove to some extent impracticable because of some subsequent action for which provision has not been made.

Terms Applicable to Movements

The producer will find it most helpful if he employs, in direction, the accepted stage terms for different kinds of movement. The cast must be made familiar with these:

CROSS. This term is applied to a definite crossing of the stage either from one side to the other or at least a marked change of position. It is commonly associated in the player's mind, also, with quickness of movement, although the expression is equally accurate when applied to a slow crossing of considerable length.

An example would read: "GEORGE *enters up L, hesitates, then crosses to the safe down R, and unlocks it.*"

MOVE. This denotes a position change of lesser length, perhaps of anything down to three or four paces. Although the word has no connexion with *speed*, many players appear to associate it with a relatively slower pace. In acting editions, however, it is more or less customary to indicate the required speed to be applied to a "move."

Examples:

"MURIEL *moves to R C, checks, and stares at* ROBERT."
"*He moves slowly to the piano, sits, and begins to play.*"
"*She moves quickly up C, and tears aside the curtain.*"

Probably none of the above instances involves a change much greater than half the width or depth of the stage.

BREAK. This usually indicates a movement of a character *away* from another to indicate some form of antipathy or a desire not to face the other character when replying. It is applied also to an UP-stage or DOWN-stage movement to change a grouping, or to bring about a clear line between two characters which the character that "breaks" was intercepting. It is a short movement and usually associated with relatively slow pace.

Examples:

"*He breaks a little R, turns, and addresses* ALICE."

"*She breaks up-stage, and turns to the piano.* PETER *and* HILDA *exchange significant smiles.*"

EASE. This is the slightest movement of all. It is usually applied to little more than an adjustment of position. It may be two or three paces or much less. As an example, suppose that PAUL is standing close to the R arm of a settee. The stage direction might read:

"PAUL *eases to below the settee, looks coldly at* BELLA, *and sits.*

PAUL. Very well. Tell me."

Another example:

"*She eases a pace towards him, looks him up and down, and then, quite suddenly, laughs.*"

Again, a player will frequently "ease" a pace down stage of another in order that, a few moments later, he may make a clean cross below the other for an exit or

3

some other purpose. An amateur cast will soon learn to associate these terms with the type and extent of movement, and act accordingly.

The extent to which "business" is introduced at the earliest rehearsals must depend on the producer's discretion. At first, nothing should be done that interferes with the player's mastery of movement while still reading his lines. Sitting and rising must be included, also hand shaking and "miming" of major business. Eating and drinking with props should be omitted, but introduced immediately the members of the cast are independent of their scripts. I find it advisable to use every possible prop, however, at the earliest possible stage; I also insist on miming the opening and closing of doors from the beginning. The preliminary rehearsals afford (after the positions have been blocked in) excellent opportunities for instructing the less experienced players how to "make an entrance," "make an exit," and the elements of "footwork."

The important thing at this juncture is to lay a good foundation and no more. The sounder the basic work, the quicker and smoother the successive stages will prove to be.

CHAPTER VIII

REHEARSAL METHOD—2. PRELIMINARY INTERPRETATION

AS the early rehearsals proceed, problems of position, grouping, and movement are solved, and action is gradually elaborated. While "mechanics" are being completed, the producer must have the following factors well in mind:

(a) Dramatic domination—a subject already discussed;

(b) Positioning for "conviction" in playing;

(c) Grouping with a view to *subsequent* movement and change;

(d) Aesthetic value of the "stage picture."

Little more need be said about (a). The producer will soon see for himself how true are the principles set forth in Chapter III on this subject. He will discover, too, how his players feel dominant, or the reverse, according to the positions allotted to them for the delivery of certain lines. Here it may be stressed that nothing is more helpful to an amateur player than to be asked how he feels when speaking a line in one position compared with another. By stimulating imagination thus, he acquires a useful quality of "actor's discrimination," which teaches him not only how to convey domination but also how to portray subservience too!

(*b*) It is difficult to play important scenes convincingly when grouping is "untidy." This is a defect that an audience is quick to sense, although unable to name it. An excess of formality, an obviously contrived picture, is the other extreme, and no less a blunder. Scenes of importance and of any appreciable length between only two characters cannot be acted with conviction when the players are separated by almost the entire width of the stage. Frequently I have seen this serious fault committed, when, say, a long quarrel is enacted with RICHARD by the fireplace extreme R, and VERA at the window extreme L! The reason for the failure of this positioning is simple. At the rise of the curtain the eyes of the audience are directed instinctively and collectively to centre stage. They immediately switch to that stage feature which has the maximum visual attraction, but throughout the play the C area will always be that towards which they will unconsciously *wish* to look. Now, if dialogue is tossed to and fro between extreme R and extreme L the heads and eyes of the audience soon resemble those of the spectators at a Wimbledon Tennis Championship, with the result that they not only lose the significance of each line but *also fail to catch the reactions of the actor to whom it is spoken.* Antipathy, it is true, is often marked by a separation of the participants—but *not* to the most remote corners of the room! Indeed, a scene of recrimination must frequently involve an approach of the characters to each other, particularly if the quarrel terminates in violence. Conversely, a sympathetic scene necessitates proximity of the characters. In a love scene the young lady may, at some point, "break slightly R or L" in modest confusion—but sooner or later the male pursuer will pursue, especially if the incident is to close happily with an embrace! The producer will encounter numerous variants of these examples, and by a process of reasoning will rapidly acquire the knack of appropriate treatment.

(c) This is a consideration that I treated as an example of script-marking in Chapter III. Its complexity and importance will be manifest as rehearsals proceed.

(d) The necessity for "aesthetic value in stage pictures" will depend largely on the nature of the play. It will be least apparent in modern "naturalistic" plays, though not, I hasten to add, entirely absent. I would say, rather, that the beauty of the "pictures" in such a play must have a greater "apparent unconsciousness" than in any other.

The need for beauty in grouping and movement will increase with the poetic, or the spiritual, qualities of the play, or any other aesthetic content. Historical plays, plays in verse, fantasies, and religious plays are all likely to demand great beauty not only of costume, scenery, and lighting, but also in the formal arrangement of the characters.

Here, however, I must warn the producer strongly against the temptation to be excessively and consciously "formal." As a general principle, the movement and resultant "picture" should in itself be an expression (or an enrichment of the expression) of the purport of the scene. Nothing destroys the spiritual quality of a scene more surely than to have it expressed wholly or partially by movement and grouping that has obviously been rehearsed so carefully (and excessively) that it looks like just one more—and faultless—rehearsal.

Admittedly, there must be no fumbling, no hurried re-adjustment of an error, no glaring technical fault— *but it must look as if the players are doing it for the first time.*

More obvious formality is permissible in scenes of ritual and ceremony, where precedence, position, and movement are governed by custom, tradition, rank, or religious or "national" significance. In these matters the producer must use his own discretion and knowledge of the ceremonial purport.

Speech and Action

The producer is now free to pay increasing attention to how lines are spoken and how speech is blended with action and "business." Distribution of emphasis (the choice of the correct word or words to be stressed in each phrase), vocal punctuation, variation of *tempo* and tone—all these must begin to concern him at this stage. Nor must he lose sight of balance in "personality value," balance of scene with scene, and the maintenance of the "general character" of the play.

Members of the cast, at this stage, should be more or less independent of their "books." Some players are natural "quick studies," some slow. Some (and not only amateurs) are wilfully careless and lazy. Since the producer will discover the frequency with which "any excuse is better than none," he will usually find it best to be less merciful about memorizing lines than almost anything else! Nor is memorization confined to lines; movement and action must be implanted in the mind even before the dialogue. Many players remember lines by their position on the set on which they have to deliver them, even by minor actions that sometimes accompany them. This is a sound method.

To speak lines at rehearsal as they will be delivered ultimately is an effective aid to memorization.

The players must also from this point onwards develop their emotional interpretation freely, not only for their own sakes but also for those of their fellow players, so that the collective effort may achieve homogeneity and a perfect "ensemble."

Again I warn the producer against the player who "never gives a performance" until the final rehearsal. The producer who has been and continues to be weak about this individual is heading straight for disaster. He is not acting in the best interests of the show, and is repaying the *loyal* members of his cast but poorly.

If the rehearsal schedule has been competently plotted, the play soon takes shape. It will be well to spend an occasional session on a "run-through" *with the minimum interruption by the producer.* Nothing stimulates self-confidence in amateurs more than "going through the whole play" at a fairly early stage. Do not withhold this opportunity too long. It rarely fails to pay a dividend in enthusiasm and smoothness of performance.

All amateurs suffer from an occasional "dreadful" rehearsal. The "run-through" with a silent producer is the finest remedy. If the players show up well, it is a tonic; if they do not, the far-seeing producer will convert disaster into a spur to greater effort. An ounce of encouragement is worth a ton of recrimination.

CHAPTER IX

REHEARSAL METHOD—3. INTERMEDIATE

THE producer is entering his busiest period. Chief among the points now demanding his attention are:

(1) Final decisions on movement and "business."
(2) Development of emotional interpretation.
(3) Detailed tuition in acting technique.
(4) Special attention to "weak spots."
(5) Settlement of all problems with staff on scenery, furniture, props, costume, lighting, etc.

This stage of the production must be completed within a reasonable time during which rehearsals must be as *frequent* as possible. One rehearsal should be enough for (1) and members of the cast must realize that they are individually as responsible for accuracy under this heading as they are for lines. Further, it must be impressed upon them that the word "mechanics" does not imply the creation of a "mechanical" effect; on the contrary, this element of acting is fundamental to emotional expression, and must possess an apparent spontaneity no less than that evinced in the delivery of the dialogue. In short, (1) is inseparable from (2) which is concerned chiefly with:

The Interpretation of Dialogue

At this stage, with a relatively inexperienced company, I make it a rule to devote two entire rehearsal sessions (preferably on consecutive days) exclusively to this subject. (I assume that my reader privately regards the dramatic society for which he produces as a temporary school for actors.)

At these two rehearsals all remaining faults in the *distribution of emphasis* must be eliminated. Many players fail to appreciate that a word wrongly stressed can completely reverse the meaning of a phrase! Judging by drama festival observations, I am convinced that this is the most common and most glaring fault in interpretation by speech.

The *nuances* of intensity (and restraint) in speech must also be adjusted at these sessions. With these the variation of pace and tone, vocal punctuation, and the deliberate "pause" are intimately linked. These matters are included in acting technique (3) in addition to :

Movements, Action, and "Business"

The basic principles should have been imparted at the preliminary rehearsals and should now require no more than final correction and polish. After this stage there should be no necessity to instruct any of the players on foot movement, on how to "carry" himself, or with which hand he receives a "prop" from, or hands one to, another player, and so on. The finer shades of facial expression, "eye-play," and gesture must now be fixed.

The producer's greatest problem with an amateur company will often be the difficulty of convincing his cast that these minor details are essential parts of the show *and must not be varied or omitted at any subsequent rehearsal or performance.* Only when they have become

3*

almost instinctive will they achieve and retain spontaneity.

Two sessions will serve to reveal any weak spots that have not impressed themselves on the producer at previous "runs-through." It cannot be too strongly urged that their elimination must be achieved no later than at this stage of the production. If this involves additional private tuition for one or two of the "backward" players, now is the time to give it.

Throughout the intermediate rehearsals "props" must be used—cups and saucers, glasses, telephones, revolvers, letters, telegrams, "swords," etc. Not all that must be used eventually will be available, but substitutes must resemble "the real thing" as closely as possible. The use of actual food (in the most suitable stage forms) is extremely important. Stage eating and drinking need to be completely convincing and must be practised with edibles that can be consumed with ease and grace.

The aim of the plotted rehearsal schedule is to ensure that the essential work is tackled in proper sequence from foundation to roof. Play production should not be embarked upon haphazardly. Floors come before tiles; wall paper, enamel, and chromium door furniture last! We find ourselves, then, applying a fifth analogy —a producer is the architect of the building.

Staging the Play

Between rehearsal sessions the producer should discuss staging requirements with his staff. Every problem of scenery, furniture, props, costume, and lighting must be solved not later than two weeks before production. The producer should avoid, if possible, accepting the "next best thing," insist on the impossible as long as possible—and then submit to the minimum of compromise with charming grace! This must not be taken, however, as a simplification of his problems. On the contrary, he must have the knowledge and ability to suggest solutions, alternatives, and improvisations and to see that they are carried out.

I remind the producer who may assume that he will enjoy occasional leisure at this stage, that some final tuition in make-up will probably be necessary—unless he has a deputy instructor. There will also have to be visits to the theatre to clear up points and to keep an eye on staff progress, and committee members may ask troublesome questions!

Prompt Copy

At this stage the prompt copy should be complete, fully annotated, and ready for use in the theatre. If, as sometimes occurs in amateur productions, it is the duty of the prompt to warn "Lights" for the lighting changes, the copy must be marked "WARN LIGHTS" in *red ink* a few speeches before each cue, and the cues themselves marked "LIGHTS—GO" in green, with an arrow-head or a big green dot.

Similarly, the call-boy's copy must be marked with warnings in red for each member of the cast at points in the script that allow ample time for every call to be given and obeyed.

The period ends with a full "run-through" uninterrupted by the producer, who delivers an "adjudication" at the end. The play now "lives," and the company is ready for the most exciting stage of the production.

CHAPTER X

REHEARSAL METHOD—4. THE FINAL STAGES

PRODUCER and company must regard all rehearsals from now onward as being, virtually, performances. True, they will not have that final collaboration, the presence of an audience, which alone can complete the creation. None the less, the rehearsals must be treated as performances, with firm adherence to interpretation by word and deed, not even the least point being left to "inspiration on the night." In short, the cast must perform (and behave) as if an audience were present.

The producer should view his "creation" in perspective and decide whether he has achieved "shape," "balance," and "climax." Is the comedic element of this scene or that sufficiently brought out? Does it, on the other hand, incline to swamp the "drama"? Is SIR HENRY too strongly played—or is *he* just right but HARRIET lacking in personality value? Is that "pause and silent exit," immediately before the curtain of Act 2, a shade too long—or a little too quick? How are these elements likely to affect "audience control?" These are the questions the producer must ask himself now— and answer. Experience will assist him. Yet even with this—prophecy may prove fallible, for what producer or player can foresee with certainty audience reactions, which will probably vary. Yet, however unreliable speculation may be, the producer must stand or fall by his final directions.

The following are some of the matters that must now deeply concern him:

Attack: Nothing induces a loss of interest (and the creation of restlessness) in the audience more than the absence of crisp "attack" and a continual listlessness of treatment. There are numerous variants of "openings" to plays or acts. They range from the "empty stage and black-out" to the brilliantly lighted crowd scene with a babel of uproar. Yet every "opening," as soon as speech begins, can have some quality of "attack," however quiet, and this must be sustained (with variations of intensity) throughout. The gravitating voice, the sustained slowness of *tempo*, and indeterminate "sloppy" movement lull the audience and deaden interest.

Climax: Climactic moments of varying degrees of excitement coincide usually with the fall of the curtain on each act, but they occur also during the action. The relative heightening of each climax is one result of the application of the producer's skill—if the author has provided the written material out of which these moments may be created! In general the highest points of climax are at the "curtains," since the wise dramatist aims at leaving his audience in a state of expectancy during the intervals, wishing to know what "is going to happen next." There is, however, no inflexible law on this, since plays differ vastly in character and purport, but the producer must give careful direction as he conceives and gives significance to the author's intention.

Suspense is not confined to speculations that are made between the acts! It occurs during the traffic of the play, and may be achieved by varied means. The sensation of suspense may be aroused by the inscrutability of a single character, or by the mysterious behaviour and cryptic utterances of a group of players. Momentary suspense can be created by stillness and silence, which can be protracted if the "suspension" is *acted*: the stillness and silence must be clearly *intentional*, and as clearly *an expression of character and state of mind*. Otherwise the impression of an unfortunate lapse of memory may be conveyed.

Last Words on "Conducting": Our orchestral analogy now finds its maximum application. At each remaining rehearsal the producer must induce and control all the subtle variations of *tempo* and of tone. If he has built up the elements of his production in correct sequence, however, he will obtain ready response to his baton. After a few full rehearsals, with perhaps one or two "special scene sessions," the company is ready for:

The Dress Rehearsal: First, I emphasize the importance of having, if possible, the last three or four rehearsals on the stage of the theatre, with the scenery and furniture, if available, and certainly the actual props to be used during public performance. If the production is of a costume play, the producer must insist on the wardrobe being delivered in time for a dress parade and, on a subsequent evening, a "run-through" in costume before the full dress rehearsal.

At the dress parade members of the cast are fitted, any errors are noted and dealt with, and the players move about freely in order to get the "feel" of their costumes. They also receive final instruction on "how to wear" the dress of the period and, while in costume, practise the appropriate gestures. A short rehearsal of one or two brief scenes should be included. These measures reduce the awkwardness that is often apparent in players who have not worn their costumes until the first night.

At the dress rehearsal, the atmosphere in the theatre is, invariably, changed. There is "electricity" in the air. Both amateur and professional players are subject to its influence. The producer should be at his calmest. Nothing—the collapse of the pillared arch up L for Act I, the gash in the centre of the sky-cloth, the leading lady's tears!—should ruffle him. His imperturbability will communicate itself (eventually) to All Concerned. It should be sustained throughout the first-night and the entire run!

The region of the stage is the inviolable domain of the S.D. and/or the S.M. and his staff. The wise producer will leave them to it, and not invade it unless he feels certain, or has been told, that his presence is necessary.

Before the rehearsal there will have been a setting and lighting rehearsal. Every lighting cue will have been tried out, every lamp on the spot-bar adjusted for "tilt," the last colour changes will have been made, and the timing of every "fade in" and "fade out" rehearsed. Stage hands, or members of the staff will have acted as "stand-ins" so that the various acting area "pools" are positioned and angled with the utmost accuracy. "Lights" has been satisfied (we hope!) and is in supreme command of the switchboard.

On the pass-door, through which the players will

reach the stage at the proper time, the following injunctions are boldly worded:

STAGE

CAST AND STAFF <u>ONLY</u>

<u>NO</u> SMOKING ALLOWED

SILENCE

In each dressing-room, in the green room (if any) and in other prominent places, is displayed a set of rules. These must be crisply, though politely worded, and be implacably enforced, irrespective of the importance or the sex of the players.

These rules will include an absolute ban on smoking "back-stage," no conversation there above a whisper, and then only about necessities. Nor, before the rise of the curtain, will any player be admitted to the stage region unless summoned by order of the producer. A player infringing any of these rules should be dismissed to the dressing-room by the stage director or manager without reference to the producer. Only during the action of the play have members of the cast free admission to the stage and they must be made to realize that "conversation in the wings" *can* be heard in the auditorium as clearly, sometimes, as "dialogue off-stage."

No less important is the "NO SMOKING" order. Amateurs sometimes complain that they are being treated as children. My reply is that if Sir Laurence Olivier or Dame Sybil Thorndike obey these rules willingly and without loss of dignity, the Templetown

Thespians should be similarly obedient.   In any event,
I never relax the rules!

While members of the stage staff are completing the
setting-up, and "Lights" is setting his opening lighting,
the producer is supervising make-up, making a tour of
the dressing-rooms, encouraging all, and soothing
"nerves," if any are noticeable.   He should never be
far away from his own dressing-room at this time,
especially after the "half-hour call." The players should
have arrived at least one hour before curtain rise.   In a
big show, with a chorus, or a crowd, and particularly
in a costume piece, the "make-up call" must be earlier
for the majority.   Frequently, for such productions a
professional perruquier and make-up staff has been
engaged; then a strict "make-up rota" must be
arranged and kept.

Not later than the "quarter-hour call" the S.M. will
send an A.S.M. to the producer with the crisp message,
"The stage is ready, sir." Thereupon, the producer
makes his way immediately to the stage, ground plan in
hand, and, with the S.D. or S.M., will "pass stage."

The flats must coincide with the coloured chalk
marks on the stage-cloth that were drawn as guides at
the first setting-up. The back-cloth must have no
wrinkles, wings must perfectly "mask-in" the back-
stage area, "borders" must completely conceal the
lighting battens and the top edges of the flats, every
door must open with ease—and close firmly.   There is
no worse "technical hitch" than a badly operating
door. The precise adjustment of furniture and the
presence of every stage prop for the opening are
checked.

Corrections and adjustments having been made, the

producer signifies his approval, checks his watch with the S.M., the call-boys go their rounds, and the musical director (if there is an orchestra), is given a signal at the proper moment to take his place in the orchestra pit.

The producer now goes in front, ready to watch the rehearsal, taking with him an A.S.M. or, perhaps, the S.M., with note-pad and pencil.

The S.D. (or S.M.) is now in full command on stage. Signals are given for "Stand by tabs," "House lights out," etc., and he is sufficiently familiar with the show to "take the tabs up" at the right moment. The opening players are on stage, or in the wings, as required, and—THE PLAY IS ON!

If a production has been built up properly, the dress rehearsal ought to be comparatively smooth. There will be blunders. Some player will "come on" minus a sword or a powder compact; a door, despite the check, will mysteriously open without human agency; a "black-out" won't happen, and even the prompter's voice may be heard. In a back stall (or the dress circle) the producer listens, listens, listens, whispering notes to the A.S.M., who records them in full. Only disaster will induce the producer to shout "STOP!" If this occurs, as soon as the problem is solved, the cast goes back to the nearest point that is helpful to a resumption.

An "adjudication" follows each act. If necessary, "bits and pieces" are taken over again to fix them clearly, only the players involved remaining; the rest retire immediately, and quietly, to their dressing-rooms.

As soon as the stage is clear of players, the stage hands "strike" the set—if there is a change—and the stage staff change or re-arrange furniture and props.

The routine for the succeeding acts is similar. Opportunity must be created for dealing with revisions or corrections of lighting and setting, all essential points having been noted at the rehearsal.

Have I painted too rosy a picture? I do not think so. Much depends on the "build-up" during the preceding weeks; also on the loyalty and the enthusiasm of the cast and staff. The producer must not forget that these qualities can be inspired largely by his own approach and labour.

CHAPTER XI

OF FIRST NIGHTS AND PLAYERS. OF PLAY-GOERS, OF PRODUCERS, OF PLAYWRIGHTS AND PLAYS

THE routine and discipline on first—and subsequent —nights are the same as for the dress rehearsal, except, perhaps, that discipline should be even more rigidly enforced.

Most of the cast, on the first night, will not be (apparently) so fatigued on arrival as the producer has probably feared! "First night excitement" differs subtly from that of the dress rehearsal. There is also a condition diagnosed as "first night nerves." Of these the producer must be wary, for there are two distinct brands—the genuine and the spurious. The former may be partly physical and partly the over-anxiety of a conscientious artiste to give the best possible performance. This is successfully treated by calm encouragement and comradeship. The latter (easy to recognize if you have studied the "sufferer" during the rehearsal period) is just "put on" to prove the possession of an "artistic temperament"—even "artistic genius!" It can be ignored—until signs of spreading infection appear. Then the culprit should be taken aside and informed that the exhibition is not impressive and must cease.

The producer's first duty on arrival at the theatre, is to go on stage, to see that all is well with his staff, and to solve any problems that have arisen. He will then visit the dressing-rooms, supervising make-up and encouraging the cast until called by the A.S.M. to "pass stage." This will not occupy all his time; there will be matters that claim his attention in his own dressing-room.

During the performance he will be on stage most of the time, ready to deal with any first-night crises. If all is going well and his staff is quite reliable, he should try to see some of the show from the front in order that later he may correct, revise, or admonish for the improvement of subsequent performances.

The S.M. will record the precise playing time of *each act*, and the producer (who knows how long these should be) will be in a position to tell the cast when they have played too slowly or too fast; there may have been failure to pick up cues smartly and the delivery of some lines may have flagged, or pauses may have been exaggerated and "silent business" protracted. The offending players must be firmly warned and instructed.

The cast will have been asked to leave the stage IMMEDIATELY, SWIFTLY, and SILENTLY at the fall of the curtain on Acts 1 and 2. The staff have, say, eight minutes in which to "strike and set" and object to players getting in their way! How right they are! "Inquests," if unavoidable, should be conducted in the dressing-room or postponed until after the show.

No visitors are permitted on any pretext whatever, before or during the show—which means also "during the intervals."

Finally, the cast will have been rehearsed for the curtain calls at the end of Act 3. The players already on stage, remain; the others, who are standing by in the wings, enter swiftly and silently when the curtain falls, and the entire cast quickly forms the pre-arranged line. The producer signals the tabs up and down smartly, once, unless the applause merits another "call." The wise producer is not niggardly in giving his company full public acknowledgement, but must cut any calls after the applause is "dead." The surest way to kill applause is to hesitate in taking the curtain up again, *or* by keeping it up too long. The players have been taught how to acknowledge applause with dignity and grace. This must be done impersonally; there must be no conscious "bowing and smiling" to individual members of the audience. The obeisances should be definite and from the waist, and accompanied by a quiet smile. Any exhibitions of physical exhaustion ("I have given my public *my all* to-night") or giggles or whispers are in the worst possible taste.

Once the curtain is finally "down" the producer should allow the cast to "simmer down" before dealing with any points of correction. He must, however, be smart enough to get these tackled before his players receive their "fans." These visits ought to be prohibited, along with "last-night bouquets," but alas! this seems to be quite impossible. I have found that the best solution is to summon the players on stage before they begin to remove their make-up and to change. Some of the "effervescence" has subsided, and no strangers are admitted. The proceedings can be brief but must open with a word of thanks *from the producer*! Who knows—they may close with a round of cheers for the Captain of the Ship! And so to bed.

Of Playgoers

By what standards are you to judge the artistic success of your production? By the applause—or your inmost conviction of what has been right and what has been wrong? If you are capable of ruthless self-criticism, the latter is the more valuable criterion. But do not ignore too readily the verdict of the "customers." True, they may not "like" a good play even when it is well done; they may not, perhaps, understand it. It may even be *below* their intellectual level. They may fail to laugh in the right place, and laugh when they should not. They will vary in this and in most other respects night after night! The public is unpredictable —and yet—how frequently just in appraisement! When it fails in reaction, discernment, and respect, there is nothing *you* can do. It is for the players to dominate their audience, and for you to ask yourself to what degree you have taught them *how* to do so, since one of the principal assets to be derived from technique is the power to employ the personality in "audience-control," for though the actor is the servant of the public he must also be its master. So, too, must the producer. He cannot stand aloof and say "they do not matter." They do. They are there to be led, wooed, and won. The measure of their praise will also be the measure of the producer's sincerity and skill.

Of Producers

A well known author-adjudicator once told me he divided producers into "those with beards and strangely tinted corduroys" and "those who bought safety razors and neat grey slacks." While admitting that there are variants of these extremes I knew what he meant.

Experience has taught me that the more colourful ones are found, usually, to have the least "work-a-day" knowledge of stagecraft. Among these are the "divinely inspired"—those who are born with all the answers. They disdain the honest carpentry of acting technique. Do not join their ranks. One producer-playwright stated publicly that "90 per cent of amateur productions were taking money under false pretences." This utterance was as stupid and cruel as it was untrue. It is for producers and players to refute the charge by first-rate craftsmanship on high quality plays, and for groups to turn chiefly to producers for counsel on the choice of play.

Of Playwrights and Plays

"What Does the Public Want?" There are many answers to this question, but none that satisfies every-body. If the professional managers knew, no play would fail. There is a good deal in the saying, "They will learn to want whatever they are given." The trouble is that just as a chocolate éclair is easier to chew than a mutton chop, so a light "escapist" entertainment is easier to assimilate emotionally and intellectually than a play of greater beauty and deeper meaning. It is wise to admit that there are many different publics, each capable of the appreciation of a different type and grade of play. Indeed, any group will support, in turn, widely varying kinds of plays. Both éclairs and mutton chops become monotonous in time!

Your choice of play will be governed by (a) the kind of work your drama group wishes to do; and (b) the particular public to which it hopes to appeal.

If a group wishes to be progressive and to do really

satisfying work, an unbroken series of replicas of West End successes is *not* the course to take. Even these when played should be of some aesthetic and intellectual quality, though not necessarily "highbrow." But a limitation of activities to the other extreme is likely to prove equally disastrous, artistically and financially. The markedly "non-commercial" plays are not always the best training material in elements of technique. Moreover, occasional more "popular" plays (of which you have no need to be ashamed!) will serve to create and increase a "following" for the group which can then proceed to interest its public in those works in which the group itself is most interested. Do not imagine, however, that there is any special virtue, for instance, in doing an "experimental" play because it is experimental.

Nor is a play great, or even good because it is written in verse, whether "rhymed", "free", or "blank." It is the quality of the poetry that matters. That transcends in importance the story and, perhaps, even the characters. This is certainly true of many of the plays of Shakespeare. (I often wonder why more amateurs do not produce Shakespeare. There is no finer dramatic education.)

Beware the "obscurantist" play—chosen by some in the vain hope of being, thereby, accepted as "intellectuals." Yet take care to ensure that those which seem obscure are really so before you reject them. It may assist you if you remember that the true obscurantist's defence of his "obscurity" is often more obscure than the obscurity of his plays!

The aim of the Amateur Theatre should be to present plays of beauty, of fresh approach, and new in form.

The Amateur has a duty, however, to make sure that the beauty is *real*, the freshness a sincere urge towards deeper significance in human expression, and the form no less compelling than what has gone before.

This is the cross-road at which every artist in every form of art stands to-day—the point of choice between the spurious and the true. There are so many *poseurs*, fakes, leaders of strange, pretentious cults; yet so many sincere workers labouring for something finer, more truthful, and more illuminating and longing to be recognized.

The dual function of the Amateur Stage as I see it, is not only to entertain (a good thing in itself) but also to contribute something of real and lasting value to the art of the theatre. To fulfil this, its technicians and artistes need sincerity, integrity, imagination, and skill.

From the producer perhaps more than any other, inspiration and craftsmanship spring. The burden is heavy, but it is worth shouldering, isn't it?

INDEX